Merry Christmas

My name is:

_____

Christmas & Miracles and $4.62

Four Dollars & Sixty-Two Cents

A Christmas Story That Will Melt Your Heart!

This story is about a miracle at Christmas or simply the awesome power of the Christmas Spirit.

> This is the story of a young boy with a 26" bike, who had a burning desire to have a train set to go around the family Christmas tree each year.
>
> This story is true. It takes the reader on a journey using a 26" 1950's style homemade bicycle starting from when the boy was five years old and it ends when he is nine. Either a miracle happens or the Christmas Spirit or Santa or all three bring forth one of the happiest and most amazing moments that any child can experience in a lifetime.
>
> Not all stories – even Christmas stories end well. This incredible story will not disappoint any reader once you mount the 26" bike right next to the young boy as he goes through the preparations and the work efforts and adventures within this story. The ending is outstanding. If it were not true, it would still make a great Christmas story. Since it is true, it makes it even more special, especially for me. I am the boy in the story. Thank you for reading it…

BRIAN W. KELLY

Copyright © Nov. 2016, Brian W. Kelly   Publisher: Brian P. Kelly
Title: Four Dollars & Sixty-Two Cents   Author: Brian W. Kelly

All rights reserved: No part of this book may be reproduced or transmitted in any form, or by any means, electronic or mechanical, including photocopying, recording, scanning, faxing, or by any information storage and retrieval system, without permission from the publisher, LETS GO PUBLISH, in writing.

Disclaimer: Though judicious care was taken throughout the writing and the publication of this work that the information contained herein is accurate, there is no expressed or implied warranty that all information in this book is 100% correct. Therefore, neither LETS GO PUBLISH, nor the author accepts liability for any use of this work.

Trademarks: A number of products and names referenced in this book are trade names and trademarks of their respective companies.

Referenced Material: *Standard Disclaimer:* The information in this book has been obtained through personal and third party observations, interviews, and copious research. Where unique information has been provided or extracted from other sources, those sources are acknowledged within the text of the book itself or at the end of the chapter in the Sources Section. Thus, there are no formal footnotes nor is there a bibliography section. Any picture that does not have a source was taken from various sites on the Internet with no credit attached. If resource owners would like credit in the next printing, please email publisher.

Published by: LETS GO PUBLISH!
Publisher   Brian P. Kelly
Email: info@letsgopublish.com
Web site   www.letsgopublish.com

Library of Congress Copyright Information Pending
Book Cover Design by Michele Thomas
Editor—Brian P. Kelly

ISBN Information: The International Standard Book Number (ISBN) is a unique machine-readable identification number, which marks any book unmistakably. The ISBN is the clear standard in the book industry. 159 countries and territories are officially ISBN members. The Official ISBN For this book is on the outside cover:
ISBN 978-0-9982683-4-7

The price for this work is: $9.99 USD

10   9   8   7   6   5   4   3   2   1

Release Date: November 2016

Publisher's Note: *Please check out www.letsgopublish.com for BK books & to read the latest version of my heartfelt acknowledgments updated for this book. Click the bottom item of the Main menu!*

Dedication

Special Thanks Are Extended:

To My Brothers

And Sisters,

Ed, Nancy Flannery, Mary Daniels & Joe

Plus

My Children, Brian, Michael & Katie

Plus
My best buddies Dennis Grimes and Gerry Rodski.

You all have been bugging me for years to write a book such as this.

Thank you all for being so kind!

Table of Contents

Chapter 1 Nothing like it—a kid & a 26" bike 1

Chapter 2 Built from Junkyard Parts 9

Chapter 3 A One-Of-A-Kind Bike 19

Chapter 4 More about the Carly Blaine Bike 29

Chapter 5 A 26" Bike Can Take a Kid Anywhere! 33

Chapter 6 A Neighborhood Bike 39

Chapter 7 Change for a Nickel? 51

Chapter 8 We Had Two 5 & 10 Cent Stores 57

Chapter 9 How Could a Kid Not Want a Train? 63

Chapter 10 I Still Love Trains 69

Chapter 11 Sometimes Dreams Do Come True 75

Chapter 12 It Felt Different This Time 87

Chapter 13 Getting the New Train Set to Work 97

Chapter 1   There's nothing in the world like a kid and a 26" bike

I was born back in the glory days of Wilkes-Barre, Pennsylvania. I always remember my home town being quite special as I was growing up. I loved the city and I loved where I lived.

By the way, I lived right next door to a silk mill that operated twenty-four hours a day. My brothers and sisters and I wonder today about our hearing loss.

All night long, especially with windows up in the summer we were treated to the same old song every night.

We never gave it a name but the song went like this: "Whoosh Whoosh Eee Eee Whoosh Whoosh" It was the mill machines working overtime.

Here is a little snoop inside the mill which has now morphed into a nice winery at 373 High Street.

Our neighborhood was unique, I would say. Besides the huge mill, there were three stores on our little block and a tavern—my cousin Arlene's place.

In fact, there was a tavern on every block on the streets by our neighborhood. On some blocks, there were even two.

It seems that as soon as I could walk, I could ride a bike. I mean a big 26" bike. My cousin Rich had a 16" bike with training wheels before we were even five years old.

We rode it on the sidewalk by his house. When his dad took off the training wheels, both of us could ride his bike. It was great! We grew up fast with two wheels.

It was not much more than a year later that I was hoping to get a bike of my own. I was five or six years old. I am not kidding.

My dad bought my first bike for me for a dollar. I knew my father had no dimes to spare so this was unexpected but much appreciated.

Carly Blaine made the bike out of stuff he had gotten at George Solomon Sr.'s Junk Yard on Parrish Street. It was less than a block and a half from home.

My buddy George Elias who grew up with me on High Street said this about Carly Blaine:

"Carly Blaine manufactured so many bikes, he should have opened a factory."

Two great junk yards were little more than a block away

Alexander's Junk Yard—Alexander himself was the dad of a great guy the ladies in our new neighborhood called "Lar Lar." Alexander had a junk yard on Gould Lane, which was ½ block from Parrish Street.

The backs of Solomon's and Alexander's touched. Alexander's was almost as close to my house as Solomon's junk yard but Solomon's place was much bigger or so it seemed as a child.

The Mill parking lot which was behind my house also touched part of Alexander's and part of Solomon's. But, the fences were high enough to keep us out.

More importantly to me, Solomon's took in a lot of bikes, bike frames, fenders, chain guards, forks, and other bike parts.

They were mixed in with metal appliances, car frames, car rims, and other metal objects. The great bike parts were not always easy to spot.

You can get an idea of what a pile of scrap looked like in the picture on the next page. I could not find Solomon's or Alexander's in any archives.

Picture of General Junk Yard with Few Bike Parts

You can see from the picture above why the junkyard workers were concerned when we climbed the piles looking for bike treasures.

The men who worked at the junkyard just threw the bikes up on what had to be a fifteen-foot-high junk pile.

Then they were crushed into two-foot by two-foot metal bricks. After that, the junk yard shipped these huge metal bricks some place to recycle the metal.

My friends and I climbed those piles like they were a mountain of free toys and we often found some great bike parts and other great stuff. We had to get there for new treasures before the stuff was crushed.

It was not easy to find bike gear though. It was also a little scary when they were running the metal crusher that was fed by that huge scrap magnet.

The scrap metal magnet filled the crusher

The magnet was somewhat quiet when in use. Its noise mixed in with the overall eerie junkyard sound. But then they turned the baler on to crush the metal. That was a frightful sound.

I could not find a good picture of an old scrap metal baler so I found a picture of the whole process of the magnet dropping stuff in the baler and the big bales being made.

Some places stored their huge scrap bales like bricks, neat as a pin. Others, such as Solomon's, put them wherever they could find room in the yard. When stacked, the bales looked pretty scary—like this:

Chapter 2 Built from Junkyard Parts

Bicycle Tree Ornament

When we were not taking things from the junkyard, we brought things in for payment. We brought metal, paper, and rags to both the junkyards to get paid.

Alexander's always gave a better price than Solomon's for rags, if they were clean. But, they did not like small amounts of newspapers.

Mr. Sam Alexander was a great guy, as was George Solomon Sr. and Mike Solomon, his son. I admit I was afraid of them all—especially when they yelled at me to get off the big junk piles.

The Solomon Junk Yard workers did not care what kids like Carly Blaine and I took from the yard, or so it seemed.

What they could not tolerate, however, was kids on the top of the dangerous junk piles looking for great stuff. We were not thieves like the guy in the picture below.

Suspected stolen bike chop shops

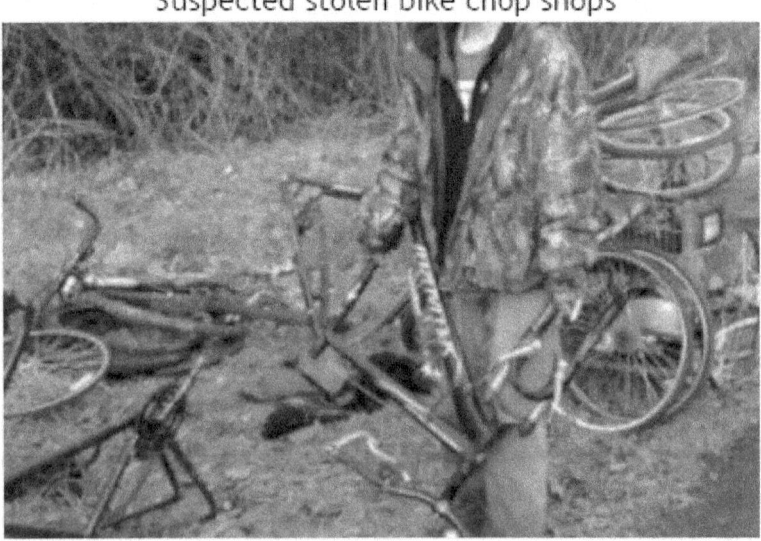

(Photo: Mike Skeels)

We took the risk because the reward was so great. We were all unbreakable little men then but the Solomon people did not know it.

So they would give us the chase when they saw us on top of the big piles looking for past bicycle treasures.

If we had a good day finding stuff, and we were leaving with some bounty, such as a rim or a shock absorbing bike fork, a sprocket, or a glistening handlebar, the men at Solomon's would pretend they did not see us.

Perhaps they just hoped we would leave quickly.

They turned their eyes to enable our escape with our loot, but they did not like to see us ten or fifteen feet up high on those junk piles—no matter how much they seemed to like kids like us.

One day Carly Blaine completed the biggest deed of anybody ever in my young life. He was several years older than me.

He had had a successful mission at Solomon's and he amassed all the parts he needed to make a "new" 26" bike.

I never saw him up there on the piles when I was there, but I knew he did not get the stuff out of thin air.

The bike that Carly built had a beat-up frame that had been painted with cheap 5c & 10c store paint several times.

If you took off the back carrier and the chain guard and you added a fat seat, gave it a good washing, and added some old blue house paint, the bike below could quickly look a lot like the Cary Blaine bike:

The Carly bike had a not-so-shiny, partly rusty, handle bar, with no fenders, and no chain guard.

It not only had rims; it had two tires with air. They were almost bald but the tubes held air and did not leak.

The foot breaks even worked. The best thing of all is the bike itself was in working order and it was ready to be ridden. Carly did it.

In putting this book together, I looked for old pictures of me and my trusty bike but I came up empty. I did find some pictures of the kind of bikes available from junkyards back then.

But no picture that I examined captured the full rag-tag look of the 26" bike Carly Blaine had made. Here is a much nicer version of the bike I once called my own:

1950 Schwinn Project Bike 26"

Since I am showing bike pictures, please let me get out of sequence on my timeline for a minute. I'll be back to finish this up right away.

As I got older, I got good at recognizing the good bikes from the bad bikes.

Often those painted many times had their emblems painted over and it was tough to tell the good from the bad. But I could usually tell.

When I found a frame for a Roadmaster or a Schwinn, at the junkyard, it was always a grand day. In other words, it was a real treat.

Here are a few pictures that show what these bikes looked new in 1955 and in 1952. Notice the fat tires.

The first bike is a Schwinn, a big name still in bikes. The second bike on the next page is shown in a Christmas ad from 1952. The tires on the Schwinn are way too thin compared to my 26".

Boys 26-inch Model F14

Note the big fat tires on this guy. If you take all the bells and whistles and fancy parts off this guy, my big 26 " bike was a lot more like this Roadmaster than the Schwinn on the prior page.

Chapter 3 A One-Of-A-Kind Bike

I have not yet returned to the Carly Blaine Story. One more diversion.

I am showing bikes and so this chapter is out of chronological sequence. I want you to know that the best bike I ever had was given to me a few years later than my first bike by Billy Walters.

Billy was my father's high school friend who had become a PA State Policeman and then a beat COP in Philadelphia. He was a great man and of course I called him Mr. Walters.

Billy married later in life and he had no children. So, he loved coming to our house around Christmas. Our house was loaded with kids.

We had the five Kelly kids, our cousin Rich, and other kids from the visiting out-of-towners.

Though we had lots of kids in the house, we had only three bedrooms so the floors were loaded at night with bedding and kids' bodies.

When he was visiting us, Mr. Walters was working in Philadelphia. In his area of work, he got to stop at a lot of great places such as a Whitman's Candy House.

I am not sure if it was Whitman's the company or a store that sold Whitman's Chocolates. As a policeman, the Whitman's people appreciated him.

Billy never came to our home empty handed. His signature gift was an unmarked five-pound box of Whitman's Sampler

Chocolates. If it were marked, it would look like this:

To this day, I cannot recall seeing a box of candy quite so large. There was something on the bottom of the box that said it was Whitman's Sampler but you would never have known it.

Every Christmas until he got married, Billy Walters visited my father at Christmas time. Sometimes we would go to his mother's home during the Christmas Season. Her name was Pearl.

I remember they had a Chinese Gong.

It sounded really neat like one of the great Far Eastern movies. All you had to do was give it a whack with the striker or mallet and everybody in the house would notice.

The striker is shown on the bottom left.

The stick in the picture that looks like a huge Q-tip is the gong's drumstick! Yes, whenever I was there I found the striker and whacked the gong until I made a pest of myself.

Out of Nowhere a Really Big Gift

One day Mr. Walters told my grandmother that he had a paratrooper bike for me just like the kind they used in the War. Once I knew it was coming, it seemed like forever waiting and I had grown skeptical.

But one day, Billy did come with the bike. I thanked him profusely and I made sure that he knew that I loved what he had done.

Big Problem with The New Bike

It sure needed a washing. It did not look new at all. As soon as I had a chance, I gave it that washing. After the wash, it was a dark dull red but there was still one big thing wrong.

Even the bike Carly Blane had made was a boy's-bike with the bars across the top and a third bar down to the sprocket.

This "paratrooper" bike had just one bar. It was from the handle bars down to the sprocket. Here is a classic Roadmaster girl's bike:

I started to think the paratroopers bike had to be for a lady paratrooper because it had girl's bike characteristics.

That would not do. I was already thinking about how I could get rid of it. It bothered me that it seemed like a girl's bike.

Unlike the two bars from the front to the sprocket on a girl's bike this bike had a big thick bar from the front to the sprocket. It was twice as thick as any bike frame I had ever seen.

But I could not get it out of my head that it looked like a girl's bike

It had a knob on the bar near the sprocket that I could not figure out. I could not move it.

I was so curious that I got some *Liquid Wrench* as there was no WD-40 at home at hand. Before long, I could turn the knob.

When I got it all the way turned the bike fell apart. I thought I had broken it. My grandmother called Billy Walters. He told her about the magic that was part of every paratrooper bike.

So that the paratroopers could jump from airplanes during the war with their bicycles in their arms or attached to their bodies, the army created this bike and built it specially.

It could be split in half and could be reattached in less than a minute.

I took the information from my Grand Mom and I re-attached the two pieces Wow!

Not only was this not a girl's bike; it was a man's bike.

It was a one-of-a-kind 26" bike. Was I lucky guy! I felt guilty about my girl's bike thoughts but I got over it. It gave a smooth ride—much better than any bike I ever rode.

It did not matter to me as much that it was the most solid bike I had ever seen. Better than that, it was representative of the World War that America had just won ten years earlier.

The guys and the girls on my street and everybody I ever met were impressed. I had one heck of a story to tell about that bike.

Nobody thought it was a girl's bike even before I told them the story.

I wish I had the picture shown on the next page to show how the bike was used during the war. In this case, a picture would be worth a thousand words. Here it is:

Now that we have talked about all the choices of bicycles that I had during the youngest parts of my life, it is time for us to finish the Carly Blaine bike story of my first bicycle.

Thank you for letting me talk about all these bikes before we move on to the rest of the story.

Back to My First Bike

Looking back on my first bike, I cannot believe that my extremely cautious dad had paid the buck and got me the bike of my dreams.

I was thrilled. He never saw the bike until I was on it the next day and I rode it up to our curb at 363 High Street.

From the Carly Blaine bike to a paratrooper bike in just a few years was something I never would have believed when I first had my own bicycle.

Chapter 4   More about the Carly Blaine Bike (My First 26" Bike)

My street, High Street, was made of small stones.

The street department would refresh our street every few years. They would start by getting all the cars off the street. They would then pour hot oil on the street so it looked slick black.

They did this about every other summer. It refreshed the look and got rid of the pot holes. There were no asphalt machines required.

After the oil pour, they would put fresh tiny red stones on the street and the stones would cover up the oil.

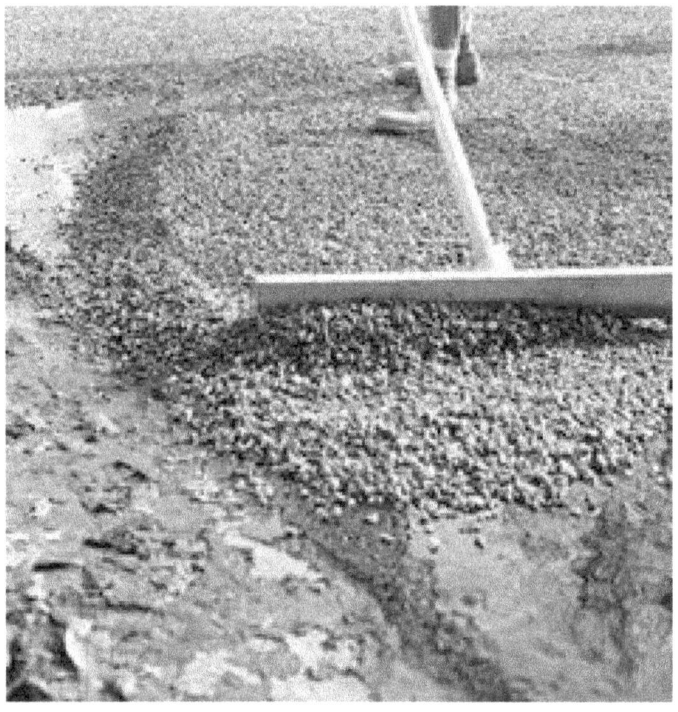

The road was never perfect but it was good enough. High Street always tapered down to our sidewalk as most of the stones stayed on the crest of the road.

The taper ended at the gutter about six inches lower than the curb. So, our curbs were about six inches or better and very ready to support a kid's foot from a bike.

You probably already can figure out that there was one problem with my first 26" bike when I was between five and six years old. I was way too small to get on it.

Carly Blaine put me on the bike nonetheless the first day and I rode it down High Street to Parrish and back fine though my feet barely made it to the petals.

I knew he would not be there every time for me so I figured out what to do.

I stopped by the big curb in front of my house and put my foot down and I was able to get off.

For about six months until I got bigger, I used those high curbs to mount and dismount my 26" bicycle. I was so proud and so thankful.

It never seemed to matter to anybody, nor to me that I needed every inch to mount the bike.

And of course, before I got a little bigger, it was always tough getting more than my toes on the petals once on my way.

It sure was an adventure and a very successful one. For a year or so, I did not ride my bike more than a block from the house.

Chapter 5   A 26" Bike Can Take a Kid Anywhere!

Off to see the world!

Once mounted on my mean fender-less machine, I was a bike monster from then on. I often think back about how Carly got the bike parts. We never stole anything from anybody.

To be honest, when we took things from the junk yard, we never once thought it was stealing. I do not know why! It surely was stealing but they kind of let us do it.

Now I know it was grand theft larceny but back then none of us knew.

I am sure Carly Blaine felt the same way. It was like the junk yard was there just for us.

I eventually learned from Carly Blaine and Joey Pahler, another guy a bit older than I, how to fix the brakes and change flats on my old trusty 26 inch bike.

Like the older guys in the neighborhood, I became a regular at Solomon's Junk Yard.

It satisfied my bicycle parts needs and it also was the only junkyard where I could bring my carriage-loads of trash newspapers for cash every weekend.

Solomon's weighed the papers and paid kids and others for recycling newspapers. As I recall we go ½ cent per pound.

I soon became a little businessman. I had my own a junk route from my home on High Street to Parrish Street on Saturdays.

I went up Parrish Street as far as the three blocks to the top of the hill.

I was once spooked at the top of the hill and never quite made it to the fourth block at Loomis Street.

Besides, the farther up the hill I went, the longer the trip was back to Solomon's Junk Yard.

A smart young businessman would not spend all day on Saturday on a junk route just to get another nickel.

As a little urchin, I had my own technique. I would knock on neighbor's doors and ask if they had any rags or papers. It was a simple process but you had to have the guts to ask.

As I moved a bit out of the neighborhood, after a few knocks on Saturdays, these nice people began to like me coming every week.

If I did not take them, they would put their papers out for the trash every week. I am not sure if this saved them time but they liked giving me their junk.

Bonanza at the Holy Grate

One day a lady half-way up Parrish Street from Brown gave me a big iron grate that had covered their hot air furnace on their living-room floor.

My baby carriage (much more efficient than a wagon back then) was not ready for heavy lifting nor was I. She and her husband helped lift the grate onto my carriage.

The twin "baby" carriage was almost full of papers at the time. The carriage did not collapse.

The papers supported the grate. Without going any farther up the street, I headed off right away to the junk yard down the steep hill. I made it.

The Solomon junkyard chiefs were suspicious that I might have stolen the register (grate). But, of course they knew me from being there so many times before with papers and rags.

    They believed my story of how I had gotten the floor grate. They had to lift it off my carriage. I was still too little for the heavy stuff.

    They gave me fifty cents for the grate. It was "heavy metal" I had never made much more thin thirty or forty cents after working all day on a Saturday. It was my best day ever on my junk route for years.

My other venture as I have already confessed at the junk yard was to keep my bikes in the best of shape and looking as good as possible without needing 5 & 10c paint.

I soon learned how to be able to recognize a great bike part from Solomon's junk yard when I was up on the pile. I developed a hawk eye! I admit that when I was on a parts mission, I always had a whirring of fear in my stomach.

When I was on the big scrap pile, I felt somebody was going to yell at me at any moment. But, the rewards were substantial, and nobody seemed to care.

Chapter 6 A Neighborhood Bike

That 26" bike changed my life even though, as noted, when I first got it, my feet could hardly reach the petals. When younger, I was always able to find a high curb or a set of front porch steps so I could get on and off.

I had some crashes and they hurt parts of my body I did not realize were there. Of course, this helped me ride my bike even better so this would rarely happen.

Equipped with my own bike transportation, eventually I began to frequent any place in Wilkes-Barre that I chose. Kids like me did not worry about bad people (predators) back then.

None of us were worried about predators. All the kids seemed a lot tougher than the sleaze-balls that might try to bother us.

All I had to do was mount my personal twenty-six-inch fat tired bike, and poof! I was in a different world.

As I said previously, my "new" bike had no fenders. So, it was not too pleasant riding in rain or snow. But, I managed. My mom and grandmother did the wash.

We lived in a great spot on a flat street that was on the side of a big hill. Our street was not at the top of the hill but it was named High Street nonetheless.

Lots of stores were close by so I did not always have to use my bike. However, most often, I had it with me.

Places within walking distance to and from our home on High street by Blackman, included some great spots to visit with or without a bike.

One of my favorite spots was Brady's Lunch on Blackman St. It was about two full blocks from our house. Brady Moses had the famous Chile Sauce for Hot Dogs long before I knew about Abe's Hot Dogs, another popular spot even today.

Brady had a steamer for his buns. He would grab a bun from the steamer, slather it with mustard, and add onions. Then, he would delicately add the homemade special Chile Sauce that he made every day.

I can't compare a Brady's with an Abe's today but I bet Brady's dogs would stack up well. They were the best you could get when I was a kid.

My uncle Gene McKeown lived about two blocks in total from our house but they seemed to be long blocks. He and his wife, my Aunt Helen were my cousin Rich's grandparents. They loved Brady's hot dogs and hamburgers.

Out of the blue one day when I was still thinking about a twenty-six-inch bike, Uncle Gene called.

It was the middle of the winter-cold and windy but no snow. Nobody wanted to move from their homes but my relatives were very hungry for Brady's hot dogs.

Uncle Gene, who I liked for many reasons, asked if I would come up his house to get some cash to get his order of Brady's hamburgers with Chile Sauce and onions and hot dogs with Chile Sauce and onions.

I liked Uncle Gene so much and having been trained in a Catholic house, I would have done whatever I could with no compensation.

My cousin Rich was there often but he had moved home to New Jersey after the summer. I knew Uncle Gene needed me to get his order.

Hot Dogs were about 15 cents and Hamburgers were about 20 cents at the time. Uncle Gene gave me the cash.

I walked to Brady's and gave Brady himself the order. There was more than enough to pay for the whole order. I also got some change. Then, I headed back to Brown Street with the most deliciously smelling bag of all time.

When I got to uncle Gene's everything was still warm. He and Aunt Helen smelled the delivery bag and they could not wait to complete the transaction and send me on my way.

After handing over the change, I was ready to leave when they said to wait a minute and it was less than that.

They gave me a zillion dollars as a tip for going or so it seemed. They were very generous. It was far more than I would make on a Saturday on the junk route.

I hope I asked them if they meant to give me this much as they did. I no longer have any idea of how much tip I got but it was totally unexpected.

No matter how cold it was outside or how tired I might be playing hard on High Street, I took the call.

The love I had for Uncle Gene and the bounty I received from a simple trip to Brady's was worth my time for sure. I often got the call.

I would even stop in the middle of a game if need be to get whatever my Uncle Gene and my Aunt Helen needed from Brady's lunch. Then I would hurry back to the game.

God was good to me indeed! A dollar or a portion of a dollar thereof never came easily to a kid from High Street. We could not afford to say "NO" to our "customers."

Peters' Ice Cream Store was on the corner of Brown & Blackman streets.

Thunsie Peters is the owner but he shares the duties with my good friend Butchie Peters, who is just a scoche older than I.

Over the years I have done odd jobs for the Peters' family. I would shovel snow in front of their stores and when I was old enough to drive, I delivered groceries in their store van.

My neighborhood may not have been the greatest but I sure thought it was. Here are other staples from my neighborhood:

Fehlinger's Store was on the corner of Parish and Brown. It later became the spot for the new Peters' Economy Store.

Mosie's Confections was on Parrish close to High Street right across from the original Peters Economy Store.

Mosie's eventually became Maria's Pizza. Maria was the wife of Johnny Hyder and the sister-in-law of Bertie Hyder, one of my wife Pat's best friends of today.

Up Parish Street on the right side was Goode's Dry Goods store. It was right next to Fehlingers close to Brown Street.

Past Goode's across Brown Street was the neighborhood Drug store which existed back then.

Our Drug Store was officially known as Colley's Pharmacy. It was pristine and had not only pharmaceuticals but it also sold fountain pens and great paper.

When we were kids at home we heard youthful accolades in our homes about how good Mr. Goode was. "Mr. Goode is a good man" was a frequent tribute.

I got all my clod hoppers from Goode's dry goods store though all us kids in the neighborhood longed for the day that we could wear low cuts shoes.

Before I was old enough to meet my dad at Kransons, when my pants needed replacing or I needed shoes, Goode's store did it all in our neighborhood.

Later my barber for life, Bob Amory bought Goode's and he gave haircuts. He was my barber along with my brothers' and my father's.

He was also a great bowler when in my later pre-teen life I worked as a pin boy and I saw Mr. Amory deliver knockouts to the pins regularly.

Don't Buy Chocolate Milk or Goodies.

Daubert's on Blackman Street, less than a block away was a needed store for many in the neighborhood. They had everything.

My dad had a book with Daubert's and Peters' Economy Store. He paid up every Thursday on his payday.

My family learned from Dad that we could not use the book to buy chocolate milk or cupcakes or better lunchmeat.

Daubert would write chocolate milk in the book and then dad would know.

Mom and Grand Mom said we needed to buy about three or four other needed household items when we got chocolate milk or that delicious chipped Pullman ham.

When there were too many items for Daubert to list, he just put MDSE, for merchandise, and dad never knew that mom or gramma had OK'd the chocolate milk.

Maybe he did know because he was so kind—my dad.

Walker's Store was about three blocks from our house on Jones & Brown. and so we rarely got there. Peters Economy Store was across from the mine shaft on Parrish and High, less than a block away from home.

Albert Peters Sr. was a great man and his sons Thunsie and Butchie and his daughter Emily (angel) in this generation are also wonderful people.

The Peters' family helped all the neighbors and were very kind during the depression. Many could not have survived without the credit they received.

Many have never even to this day been able to repay all they received.

Nick and Mary Nick Solomon had a storefront on their home half block from our home. They had lots of bicycles and parts in that store. It looked like they might have even had some electric trains.

The store never opened for business while I was living on High Street.

Irene Solomon was their daughter and she is my buddy today. I just love her as do many in my family as well as George Elias and of course her husband, Ralph and son Ralph and family.

Her name is now Irene Jachimiak and she is married to Ralph.

There were always neat things happening in the 'hood. Some were not legal.

For example, Irene's brother, Ace, ran card games out of the basement of Mosie Sallit's store (after it had closed for good).

He was raided several times by the State Police. That was exciting.

As noted above, while I was growing up, my grandmother would religiously take me up to Goode's store for a brand new pair of clodhoppers, but not until my old pair had holes in the bottom middle or had lost their soles.

My mother told me that I always used to say: "Mr. Doodie is a dood man." Karl Goode was a good man as were most of the fine men and women in our neighborhood. What a great life.

High Street was a great neighborhood. A kid with a 26" bike could go anywhere from there.

Chapter 7   Change for a Nickel?

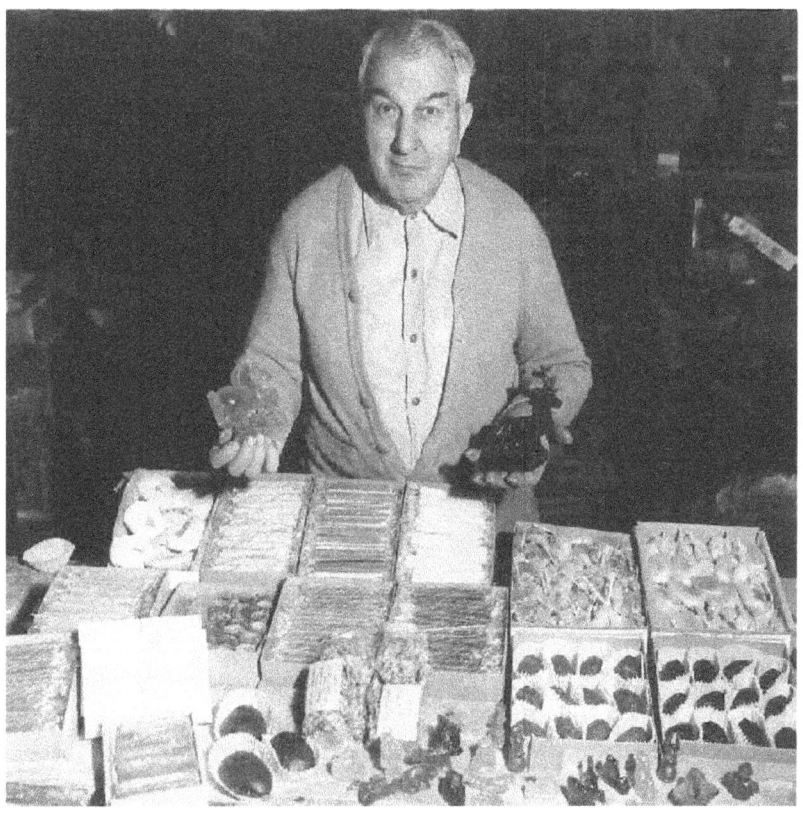

Mike Barrouk, Greg Barrouk's Great Grandfather (Greg is a former Wilkes-Barre City Official.), ran a phenomenal candy store on High Street when I was just a young kid.

It probably was a much more important store in High Street's earlier days. The picture above is Of Sam's Candy Store with Sam in the picture at his counter. It was a lot like Mike Barrouk's store.

Mr. Barrouk was an endearing man. He had penny candy galore when I was growing up. The many varieties were behind glass counters that only Mr. Barrouk could reach.

I had the same dreaming eyes as the kid in this circa 1950 picture of a candy store counter in Chicago.

When I would go into the store, there were always a few Syrian gentlemen there on chairs smoking cigars. I would go in for either candy or change.

Sometimes my family members-typically uncles or aunts from out of town-would ask me as a youngster to go to Mike Barrouk's store to get them some change.

I still do not know why they did that. Maybe I had to get them cigarettes also.

The store was less than a half block from my house. In this story about Mike Barrouk's store, I was even younger than when Carly Blaine built my first bike.

Two houses separated my house from the candy store. It was great. When I was first permitted to go there. Mike Barrouk always seemed to like it when I came in. I liked him too!

The store always smelled like old cigar smoke with a slight hint of candy confections. If it were not for the candy behind the glass, it would have had little appeal to a kid such as myself.

One day, I figured I needed some change myself. In fact, what I needed was more change than I had because I knew the more change a person had, the more things they could buy.

I was beginning to learn about economics and individual supply and demand.

I did not fully comprehend the value of a coin yet because dimes were smaller than nickels yet were worth more.

I knew that, other than that pesky dime, the big coins were always worth more than the little coins.

So I figured on this particular day, I would put into work my plan of action to get more change into play at Mike Barrouk's "Candy" store.

I went to the counter and Mike Barrouk was there expecting me to ask for candy or change. He was very patient. I asked for change. He said "What would you like change for?" I had a nickel.

I said "I would like this nickel changed into a quarter." I knew that if I got the quarter, I could get two dimes and a nickel for the quarter in a subsequent round of change.

Just then, you could hear a pin drop in the store. Other cigar smoking individuals had heard my request.

Mike knew I was too young to be kidding or trying to cheat him, so he asked his friends if they heard what I said and they all got a good laugh about it.

I was perplexed and did not know why they were laughing. When the laughter died down, Mr. Barrouk took the time to explain the value of coins to me.

He did not get mad or as we say today, "angry."

He was a good guy. High Street was a great place to grow up. I left with my nickel still trying to figure it all out. No aunt or uncle had sent me on that "change" mission.

Chapter 8 -- We Had Two 5 & 10 Cent Stores

5c & 10c Store like Huntzingers

When we were looking for neat things to buy in our neighborhood or close by, Huntzinger's 5 &

10c store was on the list. It was on Hazle Street. The Barney Street 5 & 10c store was another great place.

Huntzinger's was a great store and had all kinds of toys and other things but they did not have bike replacement parts or anything intricate about bikes.

Years after I got my first bike, when I was thirteen, I was hired by Huntzinger's for their stockroom.

When football season began that year, I could not make my work schedules at the store and they would not alter the schedule. So we mutually agreed that I would not work there anymore.

The Barney Street 5 & 10c was well below High street into South Wilkes-Barre. To get to either Huntzinger's or the Barney Street 5 & 10c, I needed to take my trusty 26" bike.

The walk took way too long. I only walked to the Barney 5 & 10 when the brakes were completely gone on my otherwise trusty 26" bike.

Sometimes to make sure I got the right new part, I walked the bike to the store.

Today the ole 5 & 10 without Leo in charge and without a building has become the parking lot for the Barney Inn on Horton & Barney Sts., which is now known as CrisNics. It is a great place.

For these two stores, as noted, 26" bicycle transportation was absolutely necessary. These venues kept an under ten-year old busy for hours checking out toys, gizmos, sports items, and bicycle accessories and parts.

At the Barney Street 5 & 10 store the manager smoked a pipe. His name was Leo. I forget his last name.

He seemed to seek me out when I arrived. He loved running his 5c & 10c store and he did it well.

He helped me solve foot brake problems with bicycles. He knew how the back rim on bikes worked and he helped me to understand how to take them apart and fix them.

It seems there was this pin in the "New Departure" type back rim that would get bent from slamming on the foot brake. Leo sold the pin for about ten cents.

After I paid for it, with bad brakes, I would often ride home and fix my bike. Other times if I thought it was not safe, since I had no backup hand brakes, I would push the bike up the hill.

That's why I went to that 5c & 10c store more than Huntzinger's. That one darn part in the "New Departure" brake system kept failing.

Leo made sure he always stocked that part. He was just a good guy. And I was just a kid! His store was right next door to the "Bucket," a neighborhood movie theatre. As I recall, the "Bucket" was also right next to the Barney Inn.

There was a movie theatre right by Huntzinger's 5 & 10 also. The Hart Theatre was just a block from Huntzinger's. Its movies were always more recent and about a nickel more than the "Bucket."

Whenever I replaced the inside pieces with this new part from the 5c & 10c, the brakes worked for months.

With all the places to go in Wilkes-Barre, I always felt that the City could not have planned it any better—at least for a sub 10 year old.

One day my buddy Tommy Mehm, RIP, who had an old chicken coop in his yard that we used as a bunk-house, invited me into his home for some serious play time. His mom and dad always fed me though I did not need it.

Tommy was the only boy in his family and it seemed like there were a million female Mehms in the house. They were his mom & sisters and all were nice.

Mr. Mehm worked for Omalia Laundry and he did well enough to feed them all of them and me too!

Tommy had a Marx Train Set and he liked it but could not make it go. I had some bike making skills at the time and I had become sort of a problem solver. I took a shot at getting the train going.

Tommy asked me to play with his several year older Marx Train set. There was one problem. It had not worked for years.

Whatever prevented us from making it work was simple to fix and we then had hours of fun. We set the tracks up on the rug of the Mehm house on Blackman Street. They were so nice.

Chapter 9 How Could a Kid Not Want an Electric Train?

Every Christmas season from when I was about six or seven years old, every Friday night, cold as it might be, I went uptown on my trusty 26" bike. By then, it had almost become an appendage.

In most towns, they called central city "downtown." But not in Wilkes-Barre, Pennsylvania, my home town.

Before I got my bike or when it was way too cold, we went on the Grove & Brown Bus or we walked to central city for shopping. We said we were going "uptown." Downtown was not a familiar term.

It was magical. While on my 26" bike, I always stopped at the American Auto Store (the building is now Marquis Art & Frame), to see the Lionel Trains on display.

Quite often they were operating them and the whole place was filled with enchantment.

I cannot find a picture of the old American Auto but, their train displays were as good as factory direct such as:

Look at that huge transformer on the lower right which was designed to control up to four trains independently. Even Lionel cannot make them anymore.

This transformer had to cost a million dollars compared with my ability to pay for it or any of the platform displayed trains or accessories like you see in the picture.

When the trains were running, it was surely impressive.

When I was nine years old riding uptown on my 26" bike, when I stopped, I would tie my bike to a parking meter. I knew there were always bike thieves in the area.

I would get into the American Auto store as soon as I could so I could make it to the counters with the great Lionel Train displays.

The American Auto store was a cut above anything else at the time for Lionel Trains. It used the standard Lionel displays such as the one above and the one on the next page. Impressive!

How could any young boy not want to have something similar but never equal to the magical displays in these pictures.

When I went to the American Auto, their displays were that nice. I always wanted to be by the display that looked a lot like the one in the picture above.

Then, when they decided to run the train special of the day on regular or the Special O-Gauge tracks, I would be there to see it.

Yes, I would wait for others to leave so I could move up to get a better view.

American Auto had several outstanding platforms upon which to gaze and dream. One was on the right side of the store and the other was way in the back.

I made sure I experienced both before I ever left the store.

OK...sometimes I stayed in the store gazing until I was chased. I stayed and watched in amazement.

I loved these miniature electric Lionel trains. There was an auto building right next door where American Auto changed oil, installed batteries, tires, or any part that you bought in the store.

It was a great American store.

When I was sixteen, my dad bought the family a car, and I can recall that we went there, of course, for anything we needed for the car from batteries to tires.

I do not know what happened to the American Auto Stores but for my money, which was little at the time; they were always an American asset for sure.

In my younger days, I have already discussed my little junk route on Saturdays that brought me anywhere from 15c to 40c per Saturday.

I took whatever papers and rags I collected to Solomon's Junk Yard, which was not much more than a block away from my home on High Street.

If I had a lot of rags, which was a real bonanza, I took them to Alexander's, which always seemed to give a better price.

It did not take long for this U-10 junk man to know where to go. To get a train as a nine-year old, I knew I needed to earn more money than the junk route provided.

I saved many of the few dollars I made, but I could never afford a Lionel Train. Lionel was the Cadillac of trains.

At that time in my life at the American Auto as I recall, the least expensive Lionel Train was $14.95 complete in the box.

Chapter 10 I Still Love Trains

I guess by now, you have figured out that I have always had a strong affinity towards model trains of all sorts. I still love trains.

I even love the big freight trains from ConRail (left) and the passenger trains from Amtrak (right). Conrail today has a line that runs through our neighborhood a few blocks away. It is up on a trestle and goes over the streets.

I do love hearing that whistle several times a day. By the way, as ConRail (US Freight Trains) has gotten more successful, there are many more freight cars on each train.

Sometimes the trains are so long, there are several engines on the front and back.

I even like the big model trains from Lehmann Gross Bahn (LGB). Gross Bahn by the way is German and it means big train.

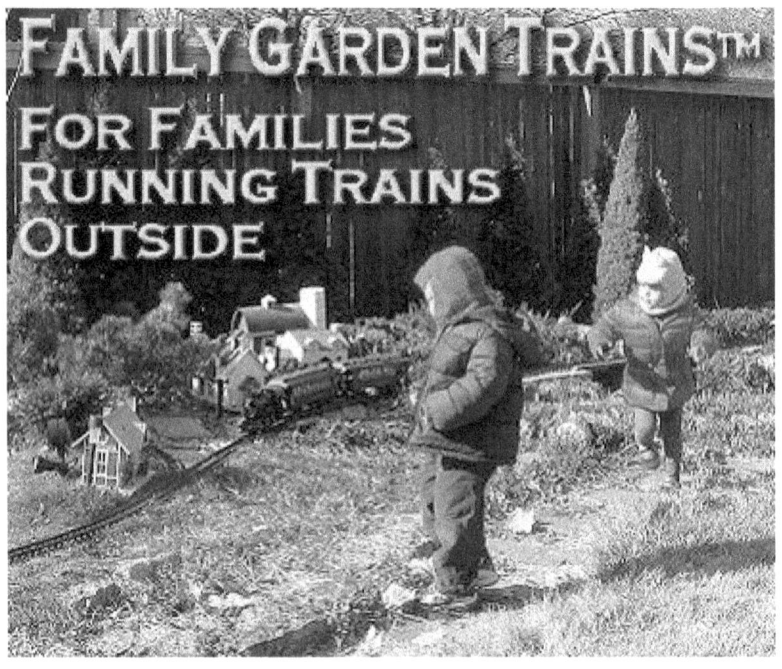

When I visited Germany in my early twenties, I saw many homes with LGB trains running outside in their front lawns and even in their back yards and gardens. LGB is big in Germany as you would expect.

Inspired by the big outside LGB model trains, after I grew up and we moved, I built a platform 8 feet above our sunroom. The train circles the whole room on the ten inch platform.

That means I have track that goes all around my Sunroom today. The room has a high, cathedral like ceiling with a ten-inch continuous shelf about eight feet up.

My choice of trains for the Sun-Room is a huge Lehman Gross Bahn (LGB) train like the one above circling the whole room from above.

Even Lionel would admit that my Sun-Room upper-deck display is a step above Lionel. The tracks look like they are overgrown HO scale.

The dreamer in me is still operative. It says that one day I should put a little automatic door in my outside wall, a train switch, a lot of track, and take the train around the outside deck.

So it would go from the inside of the sunroom on one side, traverse the whole deck outside and then come back with another switch so it can resume circular operations on the other side of the room.

Right now, this is not a secret plan or an idea but it is a dream of mine and who knows? Sometimes, when I get serious about a dream, it comes true.

No great implementation plan ever begins without a great idea and a great design.

Europe Loves Little and Big Trains

When I went to Europe with two friends in the early 1970's, we had purchased a Eurail Pass. (They are still available and are still a deal.)

Our pass cost us $125.00 each in 1974. This gave the three of us unlimited rail travel throughout Europe for three weeks.

We traveled through eight different countries, often sleeping on the train at night to save on hotel expenses.

We were as far north as Copenhagen, Denmark and as far south as Rome Italy. The trains were erste classe (first class). That is where I saw the outdoor LGB trains in action for the first time.

I recently took an Amtrak train to Myrtle Beach from Philadelphia with a stop off 100 miles out of town in Florence where we rented a car the rest of the way.

I wrote a book about it called *Take the Train to Myrtle Beach*.

On another occasion, I took the Auto Train from Lorton, Virginia to Sanford, Florida. This was another great train experience.

Being a model train buff for so many years, I could not help drift into thoughts about that Amtrak train trip to "Myrtle Beach."

One day I hope passenger train travel in the US will be back.

If the US built the best high speed rail system as implemented in other countries, and it went from Washington, DC to San Francisco, California, a passenger could go cross country in less than eight hours. I say: "Let's do it!"

Chapter 11 Sometimes Dreams Do Come True

One day, I got my train—the story of a dream fulfilled. It was a Marx Train, not a Lionel or an LGB, but it was a dandy.

Here is that story. It is one of my favorite stories about the goodness of Wilkes-Barre and it is 100% true. I'll be telling about what happened in this chapter and the next.

For me, these were the glory days of my city.

How could a kid—like me—ever achieve a lifetime dream before becoming a teenager?

Where did I get the money?

First of all, I had more money in my pocket than ever in my life. Secondly, I believe that God wanted me to have a train. How did I get my huge personal wad of cash? I was industrious for sure.

I had a total of $4.62 cents jammed into my front pocket in a wad. I had gotten the bankroll from my normal junk route but I needed more that year to have a shot at a train.

I sold and delivered homemade ice cream cakes for Peters' Ice Cream Store and I had some success doing that.

Also, in November, it had begun to snow in Wilkes-Barre so I tucked some more away after shoveling some sidewalks. Peters' Ice Cream was my prime location.

Still I knew that I needed something more this Christmas to have a shot at getting a train. I developed a unique plan for a nine-year old entrepreneur.

To execute the plan, I took my trusty 26" bike up to Huntzinger's store on Hazle Street and I bought some *"stuff"* to use to create something to get that extra pocket money.

The plan was to build something nice that I could then sell to the neighbors.

I bought some ribbon, some holly beads and some pine cones. With this, some rubber bands and a few bobby pins from my mother's stash, I made several lady's corsages.

The corsages looked pretty nice. In retrospect, I had forgotten a pin but the item was accepted even without the pin.

Unfortunately, I made just one sale, though I had put in a lot of effort and time trying to sell more.

I still remember that Abe Solomon on Parrish Street bought the corsage for his pretty daughter. I charged 50c for the corsage. They liked it.

That 50c paid for every corsage I made even those I had not sold and I still had a few nickels left over. It could have been a lot worse if I had no sales. Huntzinger's was a reasonable store.

I gave my mom and my older sister Nancy the other corsages as Christmas gifts. I then froze my finances for my last trip uptown.

I would not have a penny more than my wad which at the time was $4.62.

Christmas is a great time for electric trains

Every year in December from the time I could mount my "new" 26" bike and leave the neighborhood, I spent a lot of time uptown.

Every Friday night when there was no school the next day, I visited just about every store in Wilkes-Barre that sold trains.

The last Friday in December in 1957 was December 20. It would be my last pre-Christmas excursion uptown until December 1958.

On this night, when I was almost ten years old, a great thing happened in my life.

It felt like Christmas Eve. I had $4.62 in my pocket from my prior work efforts and good fortune. I was hoping to catch a real bargain on an electric train and I hoped it would be a Lionel.

I got on my 26" bike and went from High and then down Parrish Street to South Main Street. I took a right onto South Main Street and I was on my way uptown.

As usual, after riding for blocks on South Main Street, my first stop was on the right in the second block of central city Wilkes-Barre. I knew the place as The American Auto. It no longer exists.

There as always, I got my "wow," from the magnificent exhibition of Lionel Trains on raised platforms. They were on the right side of the store and in the back of the store.

The prices had not gone down and there were no deals.

As usual, the least expensive Lionel Train was $14.99. My $4.62 in my front pocket would probably have to go back in my dresser drawer for another year. Lionel was out of my price range.

After this unrequited satiation, I browsed awhile longer but eventually left the store. My next stop would be "Bushels" of Bargains or just "Bushels" as we called it.

It was in a huge building right next door to The American Auto. I didn't even have to move the bike to check out their toys and trains.

Bushels often had bargains even on trains. But, when I had ever been there in the past, I was not prepared with enough money to buy anything.

I do not remember what I found that night at Bushels but I know that I moved on. I loved to see all the train exhibits in various stores in succession. If my bike was willing, so was I.

I got on the 26" bike again and passed Northampton Street on the same side as the American Auto. This took me to the first block of South Main Street.

The Rea and Derick Drug store was my next stop.

They always had a few trains available that they advertised in the local papers.

Their ads were very inviting but there was nothing there on this night. So, I went back to the corner and crossed South Main at the light.

I then stopped at Lazarus' on the opposite side of Rea and Derick. as I did many other times just in case I might find something.

However, the Lazarus Store's toy department was not built to attract older kids like me as I was 9. They had a lot of toys for little boys and girls.

Rarely was there a train but it was worth a look. Little kids liked the Lazarus' store. When I was a kid, I liked it also!

On this particular night, however, I did have a few bucks in my pocket. I felt a bit different than when I was just window shopping.

I had been hoping that I might find something in a store after ruling out American Auto. I could not afford American Auto.

I left Lazarus' empty-handed but I still had one more place to go.

Eventually I made it to Neisner Brothers further down South Main Street towards Public Square from the Lazarus Department Store.

In Wilkes-Barre, Neisner's was right before the Boston Store, Woolworths, and Kresge's. Neisner Brothers' Store was more than a full block up from the American Auto on the opposite side of the street.

Most of us just called this combination 5c & 10c *Department* Store, "Neisner's."

My Aunt Ruth McKeown ran the "Center Fountain" at Neisner's and many times I had a pizza or a soda that Aunt Ruth rang up in the center store fountain register.

It was always great to see Aunt Ruth and the pizza was good too!

Here are pictures of the front of the store followed by the huge side fountain at Neisner's. It was very large. Today we might call it a Luncheonette. It had everything in those days.

Neisner Brothers store will play a big role in the rest of this story so I am pleased to show another picture of a different Neisner's store bustling with shoppers clamoring to get in:

On my many trips, uptown during December, I had checked out the less expensive trains at Neisner's. I knew their Marx Trains were substantially less expensive than Lionel.

Yet, I had never checked to see exactly how much it would cost for a full set.

Marx was not as spiffy as Lionel but my buddy Tommy Mehm's train was a Marx and we had a lot of fun with it. Tommy's Marx Train had a steam engine pulling the load like the one below:

Notice the front and back wheels on the engine were not included with this Marx model and the plastic mold was not well formed. But, it worked for Tommy and I and it was great to play with.

You can see from the picture that Marx trains of the 1957 era were not as exact replicas of real trains as was the Lionel line. But, they were still trains and they were still exciting.

I had resigned myself that if I could find any electric train that I could afford, and it was a Marx or American Flier or anything else, I would be happy to bring it home that night. My *bogey* of course was just $4.62.

I figured even if I could not get a Marx Train, it was so close to Christmas that I would at least be able to check them out at their lowest prices.

I was getting ready to dream for another year. The total of my wealth was right there in a big wad in my pocket. I knew for sure it would not get me a Lionel Train even if Neisner's had one for sale.

I find it very hard to give up on any idea even if to others it may be just a dream.

Chapter 12   It Felt Different This Time

A handsome wad of cash-- $4.62 or more maybe

I remember that on this night, I felt a little differently about everything. I cannot explain it. I had some hope because I knew that $4.62 in my pocket was not just a buck plus a few dimes.

It was real money and it had taken a lot of time to earn it.

The constant $14.95 price for Lionel's starter train at American Auto was a big setback for a kid with a wad of dough burning a hole in his pocket. But, as soon as I mounted my 26" special bike, I knew I would be OK.

Perhaps that night something good would happen, and with $4.62, I was ready just in case it did. But even I, with my glowing anticipating eyes, would never have expected what happened that night.

All the while, my trusty 26" bike was waiting for me just outside of Neisner's store.

When I went into the Neisner Brothers' store on December 20, 1957, I did not even stop at the first-floor Fountain for a coke.

I wanted to have all my funds available. I went right down the steps to where the toys and trains were sold.

It was almost closing time and the basement seemed a little darker than usual. There seemed to be no customers and no sales personnel in the Neisner's basement that night. It was "dead."

I went around to the train displays and I looked longingly as I always did at the boxed Marx trains.

There was enough train showing to make them look almost as glorious as the Lionel's that I had just seen at the American Auto Store.

I was very disappointed to discover that the least expensive Marx boxed model was priced at $8.99. It was lots less than a Lionel but still too much for me.

I had never priced them—more than likely because my big plan was to buy a Lionel one day.

I did have $4.62 so I thought I had a shot at a Marx Train but now even this did not seem like it could possibly happen until at least 1958.

I had bought a lot of trains many times in my dreams but it was pretty obvious that dream was not going to happen for real that night.

I started to think about how I always had dreamed about a train, and yet I still had no train.

It had never happened for real before and I was beginning to get comfortable with the idea that I would have to wait another year or more for this dream to ever come true.

Ready to accept disappointment

Though lots less expensive than the Lionel's, I realized that unless Neisner's had a special model under the counters, I still could not afford any train—even at Neisner's lower prices.

But, I kept browsing, nonetheless. I enjoyed just looking at trains and platform stuff.

I had been disappointed before. So, maybe next year I would save up enough! I had made myself OK with how I figured it was going to end. That's the way it had always been.

Why Is the Manager Coming Towards Me?

Then, out of the semi darkness a man who looked like he could be the store manager came from nowhere right up to me and he asked if he could help me. Was he serious?

Most stores did not seem to like a kid hanging around a lot of neat-looking loose toys. I suspected his visit had to do with being concerned that something might be stolen.

Yet, this gentleman looked like he wanted to help me find what I wanted. He reminded me of Leo at the 5c & 10c. He looked like a regular store guy but he did not act that way.

I told the man that I was looking for a train but there were none there on display that I could afford.

He did not react to my answer but instead, he simply and gently asked me how much money I had to spend.

I knew I had just $4.62 and that is what I told the man. I expected him to walk way but he did not.

Instead, he looked me in the eye and he reached down and pulled a huge Marx Train box out from under one of the counters. It already had a load of track in it and a transformer; but nothing else. It was not really a new train set.

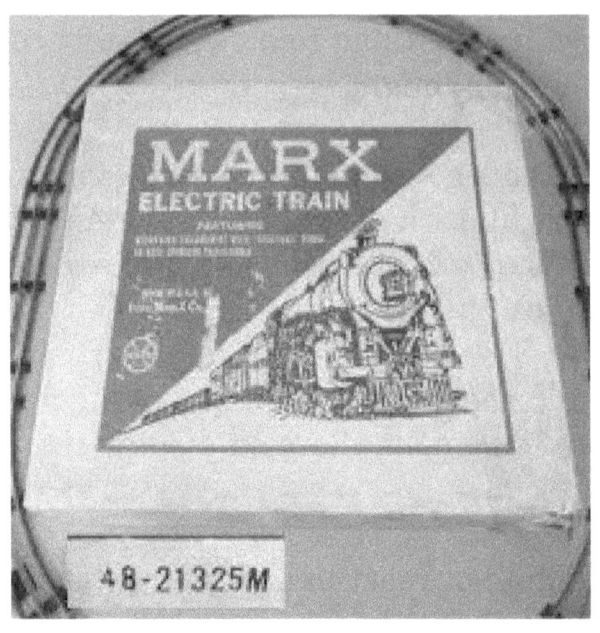

Was this man really an angel?

He asked me to come along with him. I was not sure why. He walked around to different areas where they had train cars and parts and platform items.

He got some more track and said that ought to be enough track. He then went about finding Marx Electric Train cars and putting them into slots in the Marx Train box that he held.

Finally, he found a painted diesel shaped engine (not a locomotive) and he put that into the box. Everything seemed to fit except *the why*?

Marx gauge M-10005 Union Pacific

Each time he did something like this, he would ask if this were OK or if that were OK. I would say it was OK.

I was not 100% sure what he was doing but the dreamer in me thought he just might be building a train set for me.

I knew deep down that I would not be able to afford this fine train as it grew inside the biggest train box that I had ever seen.

And, in case you may not recall, I was sort of an American Auto expert.

He then looked puzzled, asked me to stay where I was, and he started walking quickly from one area to another. Then, he came back to me with a red Pullman (Passenger) train car.

He said, "I cannot find a caboose but this car looks an awful lot like a caboose. Will this car be OK to use as a caboose?" I said sure. It looked just like the car below.

He then closed the box and took it to the register. He was also the guy at the register. He had built a whole train set from pieces while walking around the basement counters with me.

He sealed it so it did not come apart, and then he asked me what I thought of the train. I told him how much I liked it and he said: "That is great!"

I could not contain myself so I then asked him the question of which I dreaded the answer. I asked: "How much is it, sir?" He looked at me like he knew what he had done and he said:

"Why; it is four dollars and sixty-two cents...that's how much you told me you had, right?" I said: "Yes, it is!"

Thank you sir!

I was crying with joy inside but I showed no tears because my dad always taught me that men do not cry. I spoke again: "Yes, Thank You Sir."

I took out the $4.62 from my pocket. It was in the form of a lot of change and a few bills. He stood there smiling and waiting patiently for me to finish counting and then I handed it all to him.

It was an exact count. He took the wad of money, thanked me for the business, smiled, and he rung up the sale on the cash register.

I thanked him again and he said Merry Christmas, and so did I. It sure was a Merry Christmas for me and my family. I could not believe what had just happened. I wanted to hug him. I wish I had.   Wow!

Chapter 13 Getting the New Train Set to Work

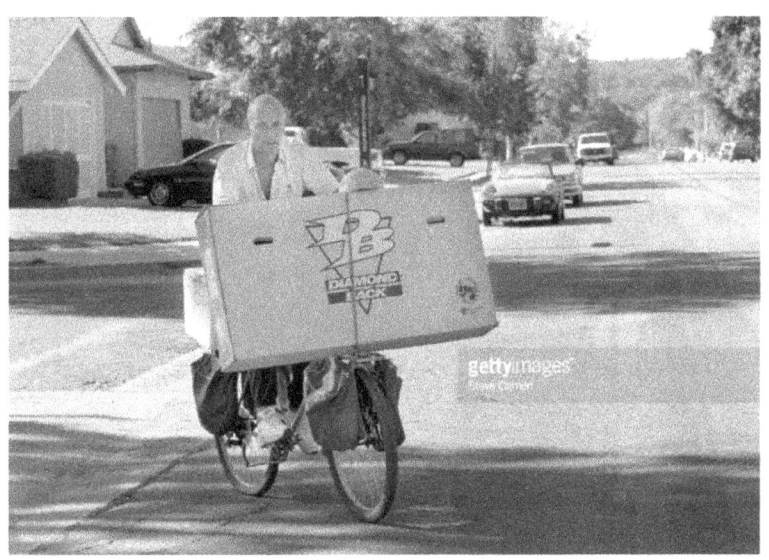

The ride home from Neisner's was exciting

Try finding a picture of a train box on a bicycle handlebars. This is the best I could find. It gives you an idea of how hard it was to balance the box on the handle bars and steer the bike.

I am not the person in this picture. I was nine years old at the time. It is not me. It is not my bike. It is not dark out. It is not cold and windy out And, it is certainly not the shape of the train box.

Moreover, I had no bungee cord to tie the box to the handle bars. I don't think bungee cords were invented yet.

However, I picked this picture because it does give an idea of my trip home from Neisner's on a cold dark December evening even though in this picture, the sun is bright in the sky.

My trusty 26" bike was waiting patiently for me outside the store. It was cold but I did not feel any cold. I was unexpectedly warm inside after what had just happened.

I rested the huge train box on the handlebars of my 26" bike. I held on to it with one hand and steered the bike with the other.

I rode the bike back down South Main Street. I passed Johnny Hakim Circle and I turned left onto Parrish Street.

I walked it up the big part of Parish Hill, by George Elias's house. The hill never seemed steeper. It was very cold but I still felt warm.

On top of Parrish hill, I got back on the 26-incher again. I made a right onto High Street, and I rode it over High Street to our home at 363 High Street.

I could not wait to show everybody in the house. I still could not believe what had happened.

All the while that I was riding my bike, or pushing it, I was dreaming about setting the train tracks up and getting the train running for my mom and dad, grand mom, and my brothers and sisters.

I knew the twins, my little brother Joe and sister Mary would especially like having a train to run. Even Nancy and Ed would be happy.

Our family had never had a train. When I got home, nobody could believe that I had gotten a train for $4.62 so I had to tell them the whole story that I just told you.

Our Christmas tree was already set up in the corner of the parlor, and there was a pristine white sheet surrounding it at the bottom. It extended for quite an area.

The train would look great running on track on that beautiful white sheet.

For the dry run, I set the train track on the living room rug. It was huge with straight track galore. It was almost as big as the living room (parlor as we called it) or so it seemed.

Tommy Mehm Had Helped Me

I had learned enough about trains from my best St. Boniface School buddy, Tommy Mehm, RIP, from Blackman Street. That's where I got my train experience. Tommy had a Marx Train with similar track.

Yet, at first, with everything set up on the parlor rug, I could not figure out how to connect the transformer to the track. I was so excited about what had happened, I could not think straight.

My dad found some small gauge coated copper wire and it was easy to screw that onto the back of the transformer. But, how to connect the wires to the track was a conundrum. I had forgotten how Tommy and I had done it.

I did not understand how to attach the other end of the thin wires to the tracks.

Subsequently, I learned that I could have taped the other end of each of the wires directly to a different rail (outside and middle) of the tracks so they made contact.

If I could have thought this through or my electrician buddy Dennis Grimes or electronics whiz, Gerry Rodski could have been whispering directions in my ear, I would have done it then.

The two wires connected to the two outside Marx Train rails by tape would have powered the tracks for the train.

On this night, I was not thinking electricity. So, I concluded that I needed another part that I had seen connected to the tracks at Tommy Mehm's house.

What was that part it and what was it called? At first I could not remember.

Then, I figured it out from recalling Tommy Mehm's train setup. What I was looking for was called a *lock-on*.

I had seen these at the American Auto displays also. All their transformers were connected to the tracks with a lock-on. Since a picture is worth a thousand words, here is a Lionel O27 lock-on

To me, the Marx track looked just like the O27 gauge Lionel track. Maybe they were the same. I hoped that a Lionel lock-on for its standard O27 gauge would work for Marx.

If Grimes were there that night, my personal Mr. Electicity, he would have told me it was a better plan regardless of the track gauge than taping bare wires to the tracks.

I figured the only solution was a lock-on. But, how could I get one!!!

I had no money at all. I confessed to my generous grandmother that I needed a part. I told her I thought it would not be much more than a dime.

She gave me a quarter and encouraged me to go get one. Everybody in the house wanted the train to work.

Without hesitation, and with the quarter in the same pocket that had once held the $4.62, I got on my trusty 26" bike again. It had another mission and it was ready to help me accomplish mine.

It was a pitch dark windy cold Friday night. I worried that the store would be closed. I did not take the time to look at a clock.

I went down high; down Parrish and down South Main in the winter cold through the brisk wind and I was soon back at the American Auto.

I knew that Neisner's did not have parts like that. I had come to believe that American

Auto had everything. They did. They were open. The part was fifteen cents.

I have no idea today what time it was. It was magical. It was the last Friday before Christmas.

I bought it and came home, all again on this dark, cold, December night with my trusty 26" bike leading the way.

Without the burden of carrying the Marx Train box, the bike got me back home very quickly though the wind was howling.

We had already placed the train on the track. So, I connected the lock-on to the track and then connected the wires from the transformer to the lock-on. Doubting Thomas that I be, though logic suggested success, I still was not sure.

Nonetheless it was time. I plugged the power cord of the transformer into the wall. I turned the transformer dial towards run.

Everything fit and the train worked for the first time like a charm. Even reverse worked. Everybody in the house was there watching with glistening eyes.

We then disconnected all the track after running the train for a long time. We took just the circular pieces and put them around our beautiful tree on the pristine white sheet.

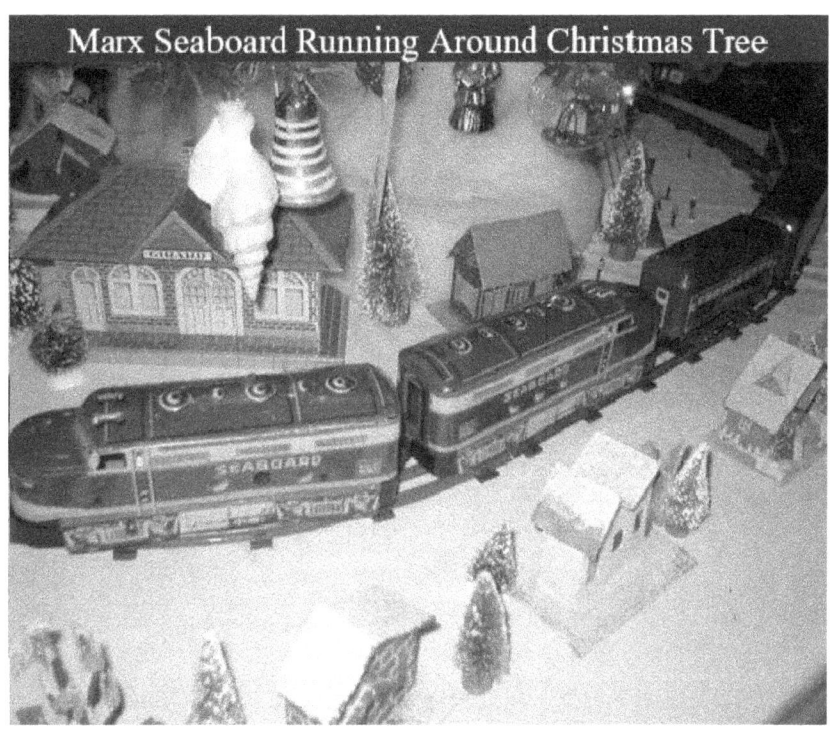

It all worked and it was like magic when the train went behind the tree and came back out the other side.

It was surely a blessed Christmas for a kid with a dirty face from High Street in Wilkes-

Barre, and a family that was in awe of having a train make its trips around their tree.

Grand Mom & Grand Pop By the Christmas Tree

    These were Wilkes-Barre's glory days for sure. As I think back, I sure wish I had taken notice to the name of the man who helped me get the train for $4.62.

    I often wished I had written him a letter because of how good he made me feel as well as my whole family. It was a miracle.

Now it is my turn to give something back. It is now my turn to hang around some downtown Wilkes-Barre stores looking for some dirty-faced kids like me. I'd love to help them get their first train.

Maybe as you get older, you too can do the same.

Lots of smiles sure come with a nice train set, whether it is Marx, American Flyer, HO, Lionel, or LGB.

Thanks for letting me tell you this story.

Isn't it nice to know such great people still exist in this world? At this time in my past life, my whole world was in Wilkes-Barre, PA. And Wilkes-Barre always delivered the best.

Merry Christmas to all and to all a good night! May your good dreams be reality and your bad dreams never be more than a thought gone awry. Enjoy your whole life vigorously and don't ever discount yourself.

Life, especially during the magical season of the Lord, Christmas, is wonderful for sure.

Merry Christmas

Other books by Brian Kelly: (amazon.com, and Kindle)

<u>Seniors, Social Security & the Minimum Wage.</u> Things seniors need to know.

<u>How to Write Your First Book and Publish It with CreateSpace</u>

<u>The US Immigration Fix</u> It's all in here. Finally an answer to the millions of interlopers

<u>I had a Dream IBM Could be #1 Again</u> The title is self-explanatory

<u>Great Moments in Penn State Football</u> Check out the particulars of this great book .

<u>Great Moments in Notre Dame Football</u> Check out the particulars of this great book

<u>WineDiets.Com Presents The Wine Diet</u> Learn how to lose weight while having fun.

<u>Wilkes-Barre, PA; Return to Glory</u> Wilkes-Barre City's return to glory

<u>Geoffrey Parsons' Epoch... The Land of Fair Play</u> Better than the original.

<u>The Bill of Rights 4 Dummmies!</u> This is the best book to learn about your rights.

<u>Sol Bloom's Epoch ...Story of the Constitution</u> The best book to learn the Constitution

<u>America for Dummmies!</u> All Americans should read to learn about this great country.

<u>The All-Everything Machine</u> Story about IBM's finest computer server.

Brian has written 93 books. Others can be found at amazon.com/author/brianwkelly

www.ingramcontent.com/pod-product-compliance
Lightning Source LLC
LaVergne TN
LVHW041631070426
835507LV00008B/553